Professor Puddles and the Golden Ankh

By Lizy J Campbell

Illustrated by John Thorn

Copyrighted: 2022

All rights reserved. No part of this book shall be replicated, copied, written or prints made for selling without the

authors' written agreement and consent which is under strict copyright laws with Canada.

All artwork and story have been copyrighted and are under the protection of the copyright and ownership of the

authors.

Professor Puddles taught archeology, and folklore from September to June, and now he was finally about to visit one of the places that he taught his pupils about.

He looked around his cottage, it was filled with artifacts and mysterious treasures he'd picked up over the years. It was spread out throughout his many shelves and table tops, he just loved exploring and finding so many treasures when he vacationed.

He checked his list of items he would need on his summer trip to Egypt one more time.

"Right, I think I have everything I need here," He adjusted his glasses and checked off the list for the third time.

The Professor was an English man who was sort of a roundish balding plump man, who wore spectacles, and had a wispy black mustache. He was ever so clever.

His teaching semester was behind him now but, from September to June he was completely focused on his pupils. He was ever so excited to visit, and he'd hoped bring back another treasure to add to his collection.

His bags were packed and it was getting on in the evening so he decided it was best to go to bed early. He felt that he wouldn't sleep much so he took his history book and began to read in bed about Isis and how it was believed that the belt buckle called an ankh was used to protect the kings of Egypt from harm.

Professor puddles kept on reading, and images of Anubis and other Egypt gods filled his thoughts as he fell asleep.

With a sudden awareness that he had dozed off, he jumped from his bed and looked at the time.
He looked around and did not see his alarm or even his bed he thought he had been sleeping on. Instead, there was a mat of reeds on the sandy floor. Professor Puddles scratched his head and cracked his back.

'What is going on here?' He thought to himself and twirled his mustache between his fingers.

Upon looking around further he realized he was not even in his house anymore! His house had been replaced by a primitive tent and could not see any food or water about either.
Puddles felt nervous now, he looked at the exit and began to slowly move toward it.

With great caution Professor Puddles crept slowly toward the opening in the tent.

In came a sphinx with a lion body and human head with a royal headdress on.

Professor puddles jumped back in surprise! His eyes were bulging out of his head,
"I was just leaving, and I meant no harm!"

The sphinx didn't say a word, but sat like the statues in his history books. Suddenly a great wind blew open the tent and off in the distance he could see a figure, a woman was slowly approaching the tent.

FUN FACT: A Sphinx is a mythical creature with the head of a human and the body of a lion with the wings of a falcon.

Professor puddles jaw dropped; he rubbed his eyes for he could not believe what he was seeing!

Isis was known as the most powerful magician in the universe who could heal and bring people back to life.

Professor puddles figured she would be able to get him home then, surely.

Isis looked around and her eyes locked onto Professor Puddles, "Man from the future, protector of the ancient artifacts of the world, I am in need of your help oh great one."

Professor looked around the room to make sure no one else was there for she must be mistaken.

"I am the god for Queen Nefertiti, and I am to oversee the tombs being built to protect and heal and eventually guide her to her afterlife, but I lost my golden ankh." Isis said as she grasped her golden necklace.
I am afraid I need this as there are enemies who would like nothing more than to overthrow the Pharaoh.

"Wow," was all that Professor Puddles could say as he thought of what he had read about the Queen in the history books. They say that she was the most powerful and mysterious Egyptian ruler from 1353 to 1336 B.C.

He stammered, "s-so you're telling me that I am in the presence of the Queen?"

"Yes, and it is of some urgency. I believe it has been lost in the underworld where Anubis rules. He is not very friendly and if it is in his domain it will be difficult to get." Isis spoke never turning her gaze from him.

"Do not underestimate its power, it takes on this form but can become quite large if needed. It is only a piece of its spirit. Go now, beyond the tent is the entrance to the underworld where Anubis collects the souls going to the afterlife. But be careful there are other gods who visit and will not be pleased to find a human amongst them." Isis the goddess turned to leave and gently as if floating disappeared into the darkness.

"Alright Sphinx lets go find that Ankh so I can go home," as he slipped out into the darkness and began his journey to the underworld. There was only one way in, through a tomb filled with large statues on either side of the entrance and somehow in there was what they were looking for.

'How did it get in there?' he, wondered. There was cobwebs and dust everywhere but the one statue that had a head of a hawk seemed to be out of place. Professor Puddles took a closer look.
The hawks head moved and hovered over the professor, "You dare to come into the underworld a living breathing human!" He screeched.

Without explanation, the professor grabbed his magnifying glass and reflected it off some gold of one of the statues and into the hawk heads eye.

"Ahh, I am blind! How dare you use my one weakness against me, Horus the god of war and sky? And I, with only one good eye left!"
The professor stood back as the sphinx moved between them.

"I am sorry but you startled me, I was asked to look for it by your mother." Professor puddles wiped the dust off his clothes.

"I see, well then, we should look together. This is no place for a human." Horus turned, and started to walk toward the bottom of the steps that lead to what professor Puddles believed was straight into the Anubis realm.

As they walked through the underground, they came upon a river and off in the distance it looked as though there were crocodiles floating peacefully everywhere.

One was unlike the others; he had a human body but crocodile head and was busy scrubbing himself with a brush, humming.

FUN FACT: Horus he was originally portrayed as a hawk or falcon and worshiped as a sun god and creator of the sky. His right eye represented the sun, and his left eye represented the moon. The early rulers of southern Egypt were followers of Horus.

"Sobek! I want to speak with you!" Horus tapped the crocodile on the shoulder.
Sobek turned and looked put out. Why do you disturb my bath? Can the king of the Nile not bathe in peace?!"

Horus rolled his eyes, "I am sorry to disturb you, but we are looking for the ankh and we were wondering if you have seen it by any chance?"

Sobek smirked, "Why would I bother with such things? Wait, its missing? Oh I bet I know who's got it."

Horus waited for the answer. "Well?"

"Oh sorry, I was just thinking of him trying to eat Ra, that poor cat. Apep I am sure of it, he would have taken this for sure. You know, he is evil."

"Hm, it is possible. We are off to see Anubis to see if he knows anything as Isis says he knows about the underworld, and we should ask him." Horus looked off into the steps beyond in the darkness where he roamed.

"Well good luck!" Sobek waved them off and continued to bathe. Horus just looked at Professor puddles who had his jaw open the whole time.

"We better get going, I need to get home for a flight." Professor Puddles thought about what he had just said and laughed. He doubted they even knew what he was talking about.

They approached the throne of Anubis, it looked as though he was not there. Professor puddles scratched his head and looked around, his back toward the throne. Out grew a shadow that blocked off the fire light posts.

The professor turned in a flash and caught sight of Anubis. A dark black dog head with a royal headdress on. He was towering over him and even the sphinx backed away.

"Why have you come here? This is the underworld for the undead, no living human dare enter!" Anubis was clearly angry.

Professor puddles gulped, "My apologies sir, lord, erm... I am only here on orders from Isis. She sent us here to find her ankh. She said you may know where it is."

"He is telling the truth Anubis," as Horus stepped beside Professor puddles. Anubis smiled, "Oh, is that all. Well then, I have it right here. I took it from Apep that snake he's always up to no good, that one.

Anubis pointed to the snake in a bow hanging from a statue.

Professor Puddles giggled; I see. "May I have the ankh please?

Isis suddenly appeared and floated over to them. "Ah I see you have found it. Thank you. I knew you were the greatest protector of artifacts professor, I knew you would get this for me."

Professor puddles was confused but thanked her. "Can I go home now?"
Isis, Horus, and the sphinx smiled and waved at him as the image of them became foggy the professor opened his eyes at the sound of his alarm.

FUN FACT: One of the most cherished symbols of ancient Egypt is the "Ankh'. This is their symbol for the key of life.

"What the...it was all a dream?" He looked down in his hands and he was holding the ankh.

"Woah! Maybe, I wasn't dreaming after all." He looked around his room and saw everything was right where he left it.

He placed the ankh gently on his shelf and got ready to leave for his trip for what he hoped would be another great adventure.

FUN FACT: Ankhs were made out of just about everything that the ancient Egyptians could craft. From metals such as bronze and gold to glazed ceramics, stone and wood. In many cases they would add inscriptions on them for amulets.

Word Search

```
U N E F U M T Q S F
P N E N A W O U P L
F R D F M B M E H E
A P O E E A B E I G
S N H F R R G N N Y
A T U A E W T I X P
N P A B R S O I C T
K K J T I A S R T M
H H O R U S O O L I
P U D D L E S H R D
```

Underworld   Professor   Pharaoh   Anubis
Nefertiti   Egypt   Queen   Magic
Puddles   Sphinx   Statue   Horus
Tomb   Ankh

- She was a ruler
- The professors vacation spot
- Somewhere professor puddles went
- Professor Puddles was a certain type of man
- The time of year Professor puddles traveled.
- what the professor taught
- Half human half lion
- Head of a dog god
- God that looked like a type of bird
- Trickster
- It went from black to...
- Stepping in this gets your foot wet
- Puddles

Word Search

Underworld   Professor   Pharaoh   Anubis
Nefertiti   Egypt   Queen   Magic
Puddles   Sphinx   Statue   Horus
Tomb   Ankh

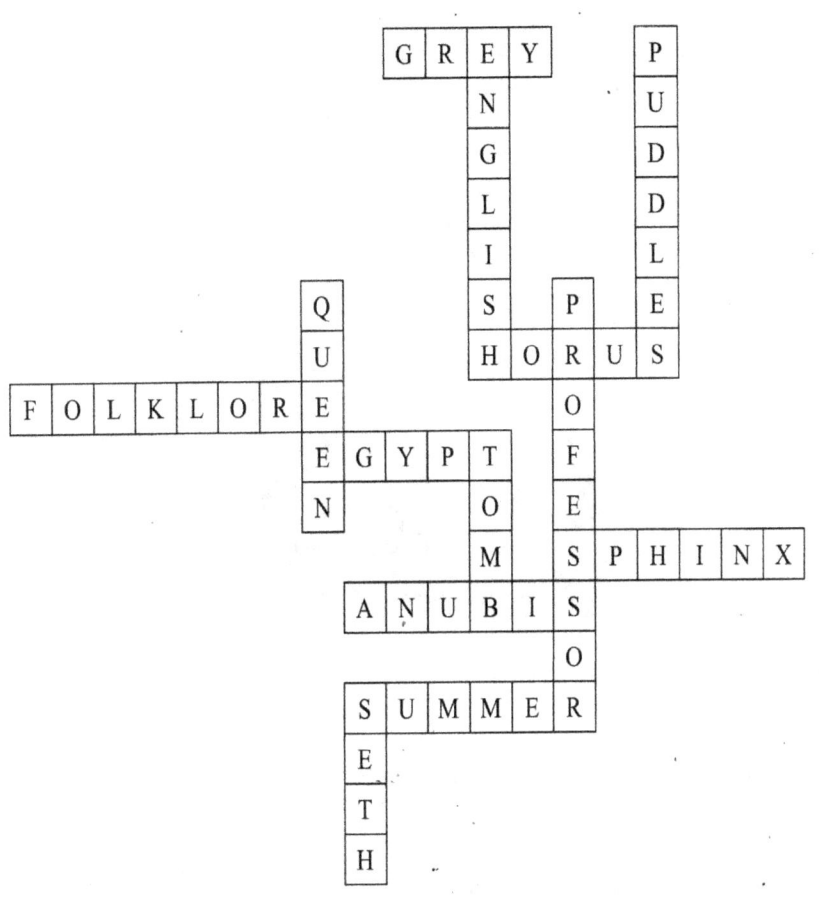

- QUEEN
- EGYPT
- TOMB
- ENGLISH
- SUMMER
- FOLKLORE
- SPHINX
- ANUBIS
- HORUS
- SETH
- GREY
- PUDDLES
- PROFESSOR

Author Lizy J Campbell

Lizy is a Canadian author, illustrator and now owner of The Elite Lizzard Publishing Company. She has over 17 published books in different genres. She strives to do everything with love in her heart and kindness in her hands. Find all of her books on Amazon, Barnes and Noble and other bookstores.

www.ingramcontent.com/pod-product-compliance
Lightning Source LLC
Chambersburg PA
CBHW050209130526
44590CB00043B/3363